The First Book of the ANCIENT MAYA

FRANKLIN WATTS, INC.
575 Lexington Ave., New York, N. Y. 10022

The FIRST BOOK of the ANCIENT MAYA

BARBARA L. BECK

PICTURES BY PAGE CARY

SBN 531-00464-3

Library of Congress Catalog Card Number: 65-11746

Printed in the United States of America

7, 8 9 10

CONTENTS

The Leyden Plate is a piece of jade 8½ inches long. It records, on the other side, the oldest known Mayan date — 8.14.3.1.12 — which corresponds to A.D. 320 in our calendar. Found in Puerto Barrios, Guatemala, in 1864, this plaque was probably made in Tikal

DISCOVERY

Sometime before the last glacier of the Ice Age melted northward, a wandering people traveled from Asia to America across a natural bridge of land. As the ice slowly disappeared, this land bridge sank beneath the chilly waters we now call the Bering Strait. This narrow strip of water between Asia and Alaska is dotted with islands that are really the mountaintops of the sunken land.

Most scientists agree that the journeyings took place between ten and twenty thousand years ago and that the wanderers drifted from Asia to the New World in search of better hunting and fishing. Bringing their families with them, they stalked animals for meat to fill their hungry stomachs and for hides to cover their shivering bodies. The bones of animals, fishes, and birds became their needles, fishhooks, and jewelry.

For thousands of years, life was terribly hard for the early Americans. Every bit of their time and strength was taken up with hunting animals, keeping warm and dry, protecting their families, gathering seeds, berries, and nuts, and making stone tools and weapons.

Then slowly a change took place. Some of the hunters learned to be farmers. To begin with, they may only have wondered at the plants growing around an old abandoned camp — plants that grew from seeds carelessly dropped the year before. Then perhaps the hunters experimented by poking seeds into the ground and waiting to see if they would grow.

Although some Indian tribes remained hunters, the idea of settling down and farming took hold widely. Some of the earliest farming communities sprang up in Peru, in the Valley of Mexico, and in the Guatemalan highlands.

In one very important way all the early American farming communities were alike: they all raised Indian corn. Maize, or Indian corn, was cultivated in the Central American highlands as early as 2,500 years before Christ.

Farming changed the Indians' way of life completely. Farming families built better shelters than hunters did. They improved their cooking methods. And they had more belongings. They lived closer together in order to work and protect their fields. They made simple laws, and worshiped the gods of nature, such as those of the rain, sun, earth, and wind. From such a primitive beginning in Central America arose a complicated and brilliant civilization: the Maya.

The territory covered by this civilization was less than half the size of Texas. To the south, the land of the Maya included the beautiful highlands and plateaus of Guatemala, and a small northern corner of Honduras. Its central area extended roughly west to the Gulf of Mexico and east to the Caribbean Sea, and included British Honduras and that portion of Guatemala called the Department of Petén. Petén is famous for its lush, steamy rain forest.

At the top of the Yucatán Peninsula is a low plains country, its dry, meager soil covering the earth's limestone crust. This inhospitable land also belonged to the Maya.

The land of the Maya

Although we can pinpoint Mayan geography and locate scores of ruined cities, we know very little about Mayan history. To a large degree the Maya are still a mystery.

What little we do know comes from (1) archeologists, (2) the Spanish explorers and conquistadores, or conquerors, (3) Catholic priests, (4) Indian priests, and (5) Mayan codices, or painted books.

Most of our knowledge comes from professional archeologists, those scientists who study civilizations by digging up the remains of the past. From such things as a broken bit of pottery, a bead, or a piece of charred wood, a trained archeologist can tell a great deal about what life was like thousands of years ago.

Mayan archeologists have received much help from amateurs — soldiers of fortune, curiosity seekers, explorers, casual travelers, and the chicleros, the native gatherers of chicle, the raw material of chewing gum. Many chicleros, while searching for the prized chicle trees in the thick rain forests, have stumbled across the ruins of Mayan cities.

In the 1820's, Mayan archeology got off to a bad start with Count Jean Frédéric Waldeck's accounts and drawings of ruins which he thought were either Roman or Phoenician. There followed a nine-volume work by the Irish nobleman, Lord Kingsborough. He claimed that the ancient Central American cities were actually built by the Lost Tribes of Israel.

It is fortunate that Waldeck's work aroused the curiosity of an American lawyer and traveler named John Lloyd Stephens. Stephens, with his English artist-friend Frederick Catherwood, set off for Central America. Stephens' accurate reporting and Catherwood's fine drawings appear in the books, *Incidents of Travel in Central America, Chiapas, and Yucatán,* and *Incidents of Travel in Yucatán.* In this last book, Stephens described the ruins of forty-four Mayan sites which he had observed while covering the area on foot or by mule.

In 1885 a young man by the name of Edward Herbert Thompson went to Yucatán as United States consul. Fascinated by the ruins of Chichén Itzá, Thompson remained to collect, study, and write about them for thirty years.

In more recent years, teams of scientists have methodically explored the jungles and plains and have unearthed a wealth of information. Archeologists such as Alfred P. Maudslay, Teobert Maler, J. Eric S. Thompson, and Sylvanus G. Morley have lighted the darkest corners of Mayan history with their brilliant findings.

But, unlike Egypt, Babylon, or Greece, where archeologists have searched widely, the land of the Maya is still largely untouched. There are over five thousand ruins in Mexico alone, most of which have not been disturbed by the archeologists' spades. There are perhaps hundreds more ruins hidden in the forests, their fallen stones covering a thousand secrets.

Another important source of knowledge is the writings of the Spanish explorers and conquistadores. Their chronicles describe the time when the Mayan civilization had already passed its peak.

In 1502, while seeking a new route to India, Christopher Columbus landed on an island near Honduras. Here he encountered a

The Temple of Kukulkan at Chichén Itzá. Time and nature have ruined most Mayan pyramids and temples, but Kukulkan's stones were replaced by archeologists of the Carnegie Institution in 1937. This lofty pyramid within a complex stone city is typical of the sights that amazed the conquering Spaniards. The Temple of the Warriors is in the background, with colonnades that are part of the Court of the Thousand Columns

great canoe filled with native merchandise and Indian traders. This was the first meeting between Europeans and Maya. Thereafter, and until the Spanish conquest of the Guatemalan Maya in 1524 and the Yucatán Maya in 1546, many Spanish expeditions probed the Mayan coast.

The Spanish nobleman Francisco Hernández de Córdoba, after sailing down the coast of Yucatán and making several landings, sighted the coastal city of Champoton in 1517. As the Indians did not seem unfriendly, Córdoba and his men went ashore. By dawn the next day, the Indians, in full battle dress, outnumbered the Spanish greatly. The natives' attack began, and scarcely a Spaniard stood who had not been wounded. The conquistadores finally escaped by racing for their boats. Córdoba himself received thirty-three wounds and later died, following his return to Cuba.

Among the men in this daring expedition was Bernal Díaz del Castillo. Díaz explored the Yucatán coast and battled the Maya with Córdoba and later fought the Aztecs with Hernando Cortes. Historians of the Maya owe a great deal to Díaz for, when he was almost eighty, he recounted his youthful adventures in a book entitled *The Discovery and Conquest of Mexico.*

Another Spanish conquistador was Juan de Grijalva, whose expedition sighted Tulum in 1518. Shortly after landing, his forces were beaten to the water's edge by the Indians. Grijalva, however, chanced a look at the splendorous city. All along the beautiful plazas he found temples with altars, incense, and idols. His most important discovery was some small figurines fashioned in gold.

The news of this little bit of gold was later to spur other greedy Spaniards on to further exploration and to the eventual conquest of three great American civilizations, the Incas, the Aztecs, and the Maya.

The Indians of the Americas were plagued by the Spaniards for a number of years. By 1540, most of Mexico and large parts of Central and South America had been conquered. The crumbling civilization in Yucatán held out until Francisco de Montejo the Younger subdued it in 1546.

In the wake of the Spanish conquest many Catholic priests came to Mayan country to convert the heathen Indians to Christianity. Among them was Bishop Diego de Landa. Landa studied and wrote about the people and their customs. His book *Relación de las cosas de Yucatán* was written in 1566. In it he deciphered many of the Mayan date hieroglyphics. (Hieroglyphics are the characters or signs used in picture writing. They are often merely called glyphs.) Without Landa's "key," scholars might be unable to understand any Mayan writing. Indeed, they are still unable to decipher any other than that dealing with dates and numbers.

But Landa's book, in spite of its wealth of information, cannot replace what he destroyed. In the town of Mani, the Maya kept a library filled with codices — or painted books — on history, religion, science, mathematics, astronomy, and astrology, or fortune-telling by means of the stars. Landa relates in his account of Mani, "We found a great number of books . . . and as they contained nothing in which there was not to be seen superstition and lies of the devil, we burned them all. . . ."

The famous Stela H at Copán. Stelae, or carved stone monuments, are a hallmark of the Mayan civilization. On one side they usually bear carved signs or figures telling the date on which they were dedicated, and on the other, a human figure. Stelae, some as high as 35 feet, are found in the plazas and temples of all classical Mayan cities

Three Mayan books escaped this tragic event and found their way to Europe, no one knows how or when. They are called the Dresden Codex, found in Vienna; the *Codex Tro-Cortesianus,* found in Spain; and the *Codex Peresianus,* found in Paris. The first, or Dresden Codex, concerns astronomy; the second, or *Codex Tro-Cortesianus,* has to do with astrology; and the third, *Codex Peresianus,* tells of rituals and ceremonies.

These books were written on tree bark which was soaked in water, pounded to a pulp, and then coated with white lime. Left in long, narrow strips, the bark was never cut into pages. It was folded over and over like a screen or a fan, then bound between two decorated boards. The *Codex Tro-Cortesianus* is 23½ feet long when unfolded. Unfortunately, none of these manuscripts contains anything about Mayan history.

During the years following the final conquest of the Maya in 1546, a number of new books were written. Using the letters of the Spanish alphabet, native priests wrote down their religious customs and ceremonies, and they also recorded their history. Some of these books have survived. They are called the "Books of Chilam Balam." Chilam Balam is the title of a class of priests, the jaguar priests. They were prophets and soothsayers. Probably many villages in Yucatán had such books, each compiled by the local Chilam Balam.

In the Guatemalan highlands, similar accounts were written. One of the finest is called the *Popol Vuh,* or "Book of the Quiché." The Quiché were a powerful branch of the Maya. In addition, "The Annals of the Cakchiquels" (another Mayan highland tribe) tell us about the history of these people.

Although these books written by the priests after the conquest are helpful, they say nothing about early and classical times. Perhaps much knowledge is lost to us forever.

THE PEOPLE

According to Bishop Landa, the Mayan people were short. The average height of a Mayan man was five feet one inch; that of a woman, four feet eight inches. Their hair was straight and black, while the color of their skin was coppery or brown. Mayan men did not shave. What little hair they had on their faces, they pulled out. The men wore their hair in braids, wound around the top of their heads, with a queue hanging down the back. The women wore their hair long, and arranged it in various ways.

Warriors painted their bodies black and red; young men painted themselves black until they were married; and priests and sacrificial victims were painted blue. Wall paintings show prisoners in black and white stripes. Tattooing was common among both men and women, as was the filing of their teeth to very sharp points.

Mayan men wore an *ex* (pronounced EESH), a sort of cotton loincloth, or breechclout. Sometimes they wore a *pati,* or square of cotton, around their shoulders. Sandals with two thongs that passed between the toes protected their feet. Priests and nobles wore the same type of clothing as the commoners, but theirs was elaborately embroidered, and interwoven with colorful feathers. The priests

A high priest being carried in a basket. The men wear the Mayan ex, *or loincloth. The priest is distinguished by his elaborate headdress and jewelry*

This terra-cotta (clay) head shows the enormous size of some of the Mayan earplugs

wore leather sandals that were worked with intricate designs. The wealthier a man was, the more elegant his clothes.

Mayan women wore about the same costume that is worn in both Guatemala and Yucatán today: a *huipil* (WEE-peel). A huipil is a simple, straight-up-and-down cotton dress, usually embroidered or cross-stitched, according to the wearer's station in life. Women generally went barefoot except on very special occasions.

Both men and women wore jewelry — necklaces, bracelets, rings, pendants, and bands that circled their knees and ankles. Earplugs, lip plugs, earrings, and pieces that went through the nose were also worn. Here again, the higher classes wore more ornate jewelry. These ornaments were made of jade, jaguar or crocodile teeth, shells, obsidian, bone, wood, and even polished common stones.

When a baby was born to a Mayan family, one of the first things that happened to it was the head-flattening. This was done by tying boards to the front and back of its head. Left in place for a few days, the boards quickly flattened and sloped back the soft bones of the baby's forehead. The higher classes, especially, used flattening boards, as the sloping "Mayan forehead" was a sign of aristocracy. Cross-eyes, too, were considered a sign of beauty. Most very young children had a ball of colored resin stuck in the hair that fell between their eyes. Watching this fascinating resin ball probably caused a good many cases of cross-eyes.

The days of the common Mayan family were hard ones. The women rose and started their fires before four o'clock in the morning. Their three-sided fireplaces, with a stone at each corner, were like the ones still used today for cooking in many parts of Yucatán

This stucco mask shows the classic Mayan profile, achieved by the flattening of an infant's head with boards. This mask was found in the tomb discovered by Alberto Ruz Lhuillier under the Temple of the Inscriptions at Palenque

and Guatemala. Over their fires the women made breakfast, toasting yesterday's leftover cornmeal pancakes, called *tortillas* by the Spanish. By five o'clock the men had eaten and left for the cornfields with their sons, who were learning to be farmers. They took with them two or three lumps of corn dough wrapped in leaves, and a gourd full of water. By mixing the dough and water they made lunch — a milk-colored drink called *pozole*.

The Maya were farmers, and their chief crop was maize, or Indian corn. Of course, they also raised other things to eat, such as black or red beans, squash and pumpkins, tomatoes, and sweet potatoes. But corn was a part of every meal every day of their lives, and it was sacred.

The methods of corn farming used in Yucatán today are much like those of the ancient Maya. First, a section of the forest was cut down. Hundreds of years ago stone axes were used; now the axes are made of steel. The brush and fallen trees were burned during March and April. In May the field was planted. Each farmer carried a small sack on his shoulder, and with a pointed stick made a hole in the ground, dropping into it five or six grains of corn, and covering them with the same stick. And when it rained, it was marvelous to see how the corn grew.

Each step in corn farming was governed by the priests, who "read the gods' wishes." There was a "right day" for clearing and for burning and for sowing the fields. The new fields were fired on windy days, and the people whistled constantly to summon the gods. A good wind was needed so that everything would burn and thereby restore certain chemicals to the soil.

The days of the common farmer were not all alike. Many days were set aside for building a noble's house, or for clearing, planting, or harvesting his fields. The ruling classes did not work at everyday chores.

After the crops had been harvested, the farmers were also put to work building temples, pyramids, and roads, and helping on other civic projects. This work was part of their tribute to the priest-rulers.

While the men worked in the fields, the women were busy, too. In the morning they washed and cleaned the corn that had been left to soak and soften overnight in pottery jars. The corn was then

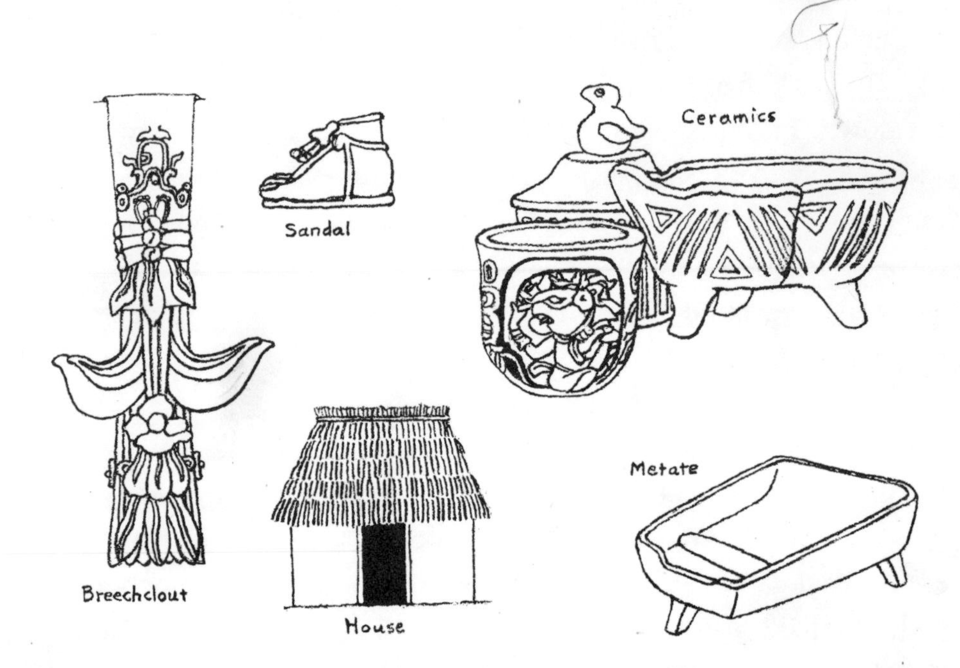

Mayan objects in common use (not drawn to scale)

ground by hand with a cylindrical grinding stone on a *metate,* or hollowed-out stone slab. Once ground, the cornmeal was set aside until just before dinner-cooking time.

Mayan housewives swept their little thatched houses, stirring the dirt, ducks, and turkeys toward the yard. But, because there were no doors, these creatures wandered right back in.

If new clothing was needed, the women gathered cotton and did the spinning and weaving. The cotton crop was second only to corn in importance.

Daughters learned household duties from their mothers, just as boys learned farming and hunting from their fathers. Probably this meager training was all that the lower classes ever received, as it is believed that there were no common schools.

The men of the family returned from the fields in midafternoon, perhaps after checking their snares for rabbit or other small game, or hunting along the way. Birds were brought down with blow-pipes and clay pellets. In addition, hunters used spears, and in the later times, bows and arrows.

As soon as they reached home, the men took their baths and then sat down to dinner. The women of the family never ate with them. They served the men first, and ate their own meals later. Dinner consisted of cornmeal pancakes, black beans (*buul,* in the Mayan language), and if the hunting had been good, rabbit, deer, or wild turkey. Chocolate, or cacao, was an exceptionally favored hot drink of the Maya. Cacao beans were so highly prized that they were used as money.

A Mayan man's house was his castle. No one would dream of entering another man's house without an invitation. Houses were usually square, with a palm- or grass-thatched roof. The walls, without windows, were made of sticks covered with *adobe,* or mud, and were sometimes painted on the outside. These dirt-floor dwellings were divided into two rooms — one for sleeping, and the other for living and cooking. According to Bishop Landa, the Maya had "beds made of small rods [saplings] and on the top a mat on which they sleep, covering themselves with their *mantas* [*patis*] of cotton."

One of the most interesting Mayan customs was the coming-of-

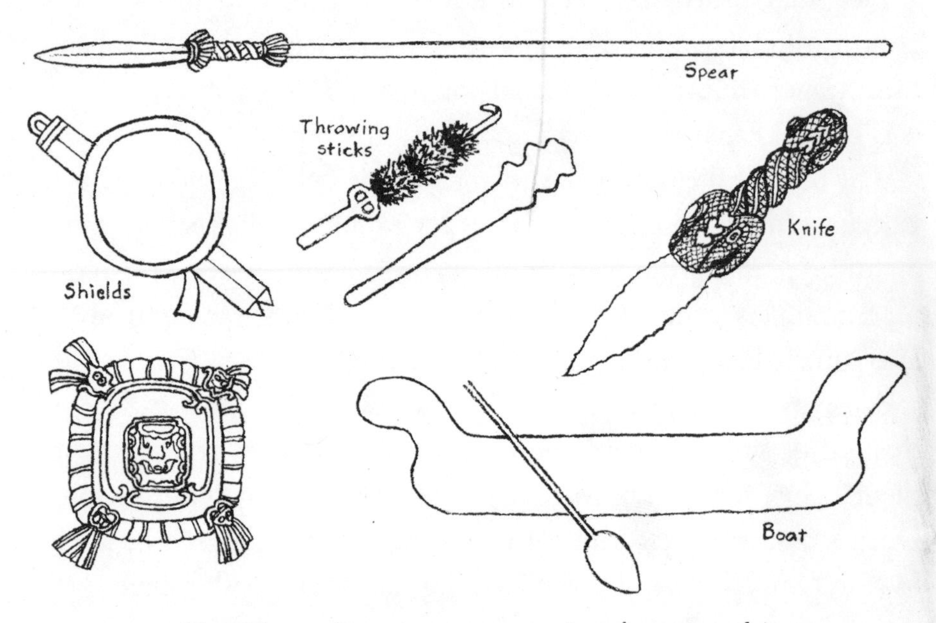

More Mayan objects in common use (not drawn to scale)

age ceremony, which was the Mayan way of indicating that a child had reached the beginning of his adult life. For girls, this age was twelve, and for boys it was fourteen.

Four old men assisted the village priest in the coming-of-age ceremony by sitting at four corners of a long rope. Within this square, roped-off area sat the handsomely robed priest with his incense and holy water. The area was considered free of evil. Within it, boys stood together in one group, girls in another. The long ceremony included confessions of their sins, the anointing of the childrens' foreheads with water, the smoking of a pipe for purifying purposes, and the reciting of certain rules of good behavior.

The most important part of the ceremony came when the priest cut the white bead from the boys' hair, and when the mothers removed the tiny red shell strung around the waists of the girls. Since the age of four or five the children had worn these symbols of purity, which could not be removed until this coming-of-age ceremony. After the rites were over, there was a great feast.

From this time on, rather than live at home the boys roomed together in a community house. They painted their bodies black until their fathers found suitable wives for them. On the average, the Maya married when they were twenty years old.

Following marriage, the couple lived with the wife's family. The young husband was obliged to work for his wife's father for five or six years before he could move away to build his own home, and farm his own fields. When this time came, many members of the community helped with the home-building.

The Maya had many superstitions. For instance, they believed in little people like leprechauns. Today, in Yucatán, many Indians still believe that their cornfields, or milpas, are guarded by little people called *aluxes* (al-LOOSH-is). In the middle of his field a farmer builds a tiny likeness of his home for the *aluxes*. No Indian would think of stealing the corn for fear that the *aluxes* who live there would kill him. Before planting new corn, farmers place *tortillas* and *pozole* at all four corners of the milpa. The next morning these are gone, but the *pozole* jar is not tipped over. In this way, farmers know that *aluxes,* not animals, have taken their offerings. The corn is then planted, and the crops are bountiful.

The Maya felt that sickness was brought on by bad dwarfs. To keep these dwarfs from a house, food was placed outside the door. If this protection failed, as it often did, an *ahmen,* or medicine man, was called. This man could heal disease, as well as cause it. Some of the Mayan cures have been described. Nosebleeds were cured by bleeding the patient's foot. Healing potions were brewed from extracts of plants, parts of animals, the bills of birds, pebbles, and fish skin. Divining stones were thrown on the dirt floor to discover what course a sickness would take. At nearly every turn, large amounts of an incense called *pom* were burned. It was made of copal, the resin from various tropical trees.

The Sitting Witch Doctor of Tikal is really a two-part incense burner. Smoke comes out of his eyes, mouth, and nose. He is holding a human skull

The Mayan belief in *aluxes* and bad dwarfs suggests that the Indians thought that events were caused by *someone,* not *something*. Everything was thought to have a soul. It was common to "kill," or ceremonially break, pottery before offering it to the gods. This was done to free the spirit inside the pottery.

When a hunter came upon an animal he prayed to it, saying, "I have need," before he shot it. Animals were killed when food was needed, but never for sport. After killing a deer the Maya cut it up and distributed it among the members of the hunting party and the town's priests and officials. If a hunter found gallstones in a deer he told no one. He placed the stones in a tiny pouch and wore them around his neck. The gallstones were thought to be magical and so would bring many days of good hunting to the wearer.

Many animals and birds were Mayan weather prophets and social secretaries. A low-flying swallow meant rain; a high-flying oriole meant company was coming. Nine and thirteen were thought to be extremely lucky numbers, and probably stood for the nine gods of the Lower World and the thirteen gods of the Upper World. A great many Mayan superstitions involved terrible happenings — death, sickness, bad hunting, and poor crops. Yet, with all their omens, signs, and superstitions, the Indians seem to have been cheerful people.

Not a great deal is known about what the commoners did for amusement, other than watching. The nobles played a ceremonial ball game called *pok-a-tok*. In the great city of Chichén Itzá there were seven ball courts, the largest of which was 545 feet long and

The largest of the seven ball courts at Chichén Itzá has a playing area of 480 feet by 120 feet. The "basket," or stone ring, on the right wall faces one on the opposite wall

225 feet wide. The game, however, was played within an area of 480 by 120 feet. We are not sure how many players there were on each team or how the game was scored, but we do know that it was played with a solid rubber ball about six inches in diameter. The players' object was to put the ball through one of two large hoops, which were perfectly round and carved in a snake design. Placed at a height of 35 feet in the center of facing walls, these hoops had openings perpendicular to the ground. The players had to be skillful and quite close to the wall in order to score, because they could hit the ball only with their leather-padded elbows, wrists, and hips.

Scoring must have been extremely rare, and yet we know that betting was high among spectators and players alike. Slaves, land, and even the homes of the lords were wagered. If a player passed the ball through the ring he could demand as a reward all the clothing and jewels of the spectators.

THE PRIEST-RULERS

The government of the Maya was a blend of religion and civil affairs. In practice, it was run much like the Greek city-states. One man ruled a city, or cities, and the surrounding territory. This man was called the *halach uinic,* or "true man." It is fairly certain that the ruler and the high priest were one and the same person. The *halach uinic* need only step behind a tall stela — an elaborately carved stone slab bearing dates and human figures — to change his headdress and reappear as the high priest.

The *halach uinic* wore brilliantly colored, beautifully embroidered costumes with headdresses that were easily as tall as himself. According to wall paintings found at Bonampak, his earlobes were so enlarged that huge earplugs bigger than golf balls could be worn in them. His teeth were inlaid with jade. The bridge of his nose continued up to the middle of his flattened, sloping forehead, and he was covered with tattoos. Chances are that he was also cross-eyed. Altogether, he must have been an awesome sight to the simple farmer.

The high priests, if they were not actually the rulers, were certainly councillors to the *halach uinic.* They were the thinkers — the astronomers, mathematicians, writers, astrologists, and keepers of the calendar. Their carefully guarded knowledge was passed from father to son, or taught privately only to other priests' and nobles' sons. These priests were also the overseers of the public

The beautifully carved throne found in Palace J-6 at Piedras Negras. According to its hieroglyphic inscriptions it was dedicated in A.D. *785*

works that produced the magnificent stone pyramids and temples, many of which still stand today.

Lower on the religious-civil ladder were scores of lesser priests and government officials. Some priests interpreted the signs of the gods in small villages, or presided only at sacrifices. Others were medicine men. And still others were keepers of the musical instruments played at religious ceremonies. Government servants were mostly local chiefs and tax collectors.

As the Mayan civilization grew, the aristocratic priest class became ever more powerful. Slowly the simple nature worship of the farmer became complicated. There were good and evil gods, and sometimes a single god was both good and evil. Religion pictured a constant struggle among the gods. Only the priests could interpret the signs and explain the mysteries of life and death. These priests, self-appointed interpreters of the gods, directed the lives of the common farmers in a never-ending religious round. Caught in the eternal struggle between good and evil, the farmers scarcely dared move without the word of a priest. The date on which a person was born was believed to set the pattern of his life. Children's names were chosen by the priests. Even the time to plant corn had to be reckoned and approved by the priests.

Although Mayan religious practices were based on magic, mystery, and a certain amount of hocus-pocus to awe the common Indians, many of these practices were also based on the idea of time.

Time, a succession of beginnings and endings, played a major part in Mayan religion. Time was believed to reach back into darkness and to the beginning of the world. The Maya believed this beginning to be 4 *Ahau* 8 *Cumhu,* which may be read as either 3375 B.C., or 3111 B.C. Scholars do not agree on this.

Time, after making a grand circuit, would come back: that is, history would repeat itself. The periods that marked time, the *kin, uinal, tun,* and others, were sacred. Each day was a living god, and was called "he," not "it." The day-gods bore the burden of time on their backs, supporting its weight by tumplines that came over

A colorful wall painting found in the Temple of the Murals at Bonampak. The top scene shows a high priest and his family performing a bloodletting ceremony by piercing their tongues. The bottom painting shows a ceremonial dance on the steps of a pyramid

their shoulders and across their foreheads. These gods are pictured in codices and on stelae. Each day-god brought a prophecy, and some brought good fortune, others bad. Only the priest could soothe an angry day-god.

A great deal of Mayan writing had to do with recording time. The great stone stelae and altars that stand before so many temples and palaces — the steps, walls, and panels, all bear date glyphs.

By studying the motions of the sun and moon, such planets as Venus and Mars, and the stars, the priest-astronomers devised a calendar that was more accurate than any other in the world.

So vast was their knowledge of astronomy that the priests predicted eclipses of the moon accurately and figured correctly that the planet Venus had a 584-day year. Many of their findings were probably based on systems devised by the Olmecs, an earlier, neighboring people.

The observatory at Chichén Itzá and the "sundial" at Copán were built for the study of astronomy, as were those at a dozen other sites. In several cities, as at Uaxactún (wah-shack-TOON), for example, a group of buildings was built so as to reveal the longest and shortest days of the year. These astronomical findings were put to practical, as well as religious, use. For without this knowledge, how could the priests tell the farmers when to prepare their milpas and sow their corn?

The Maya had two calendars — one that was for the solar, or civil, year and one that was sacred. The civil year contained eighteen months of twenty days each, or 360 days in all. Added to this

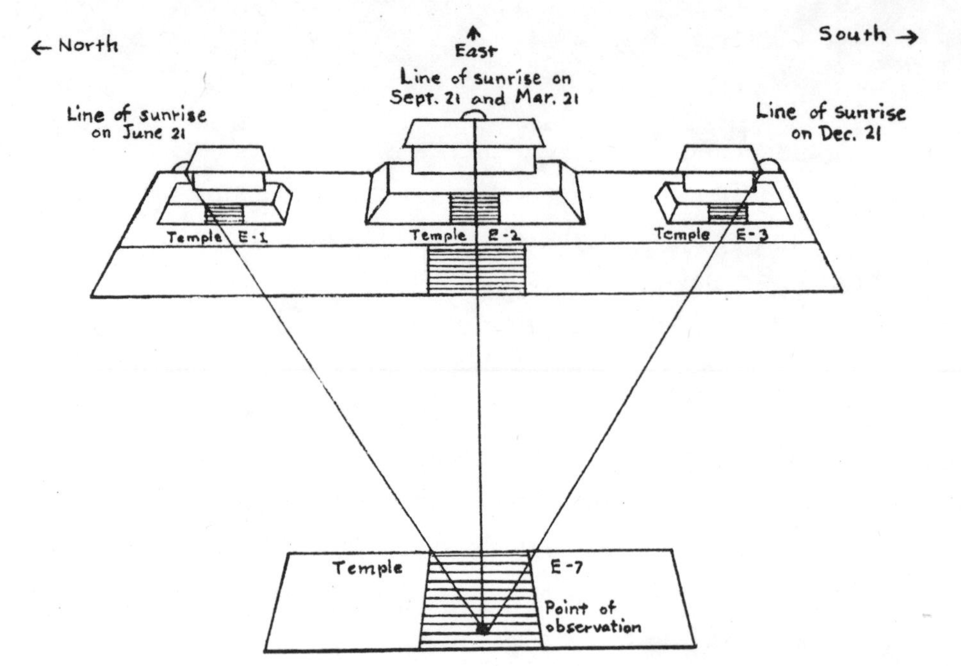

Diagram of the Plaza of Group E, Uaxactún, Petén. By taking certain sights from Pyramid E-7, the Mayan priest-astronomers were able to determine the longest and shortest days of the year

were five unlucky days called *Uayeb,* making a total of 365 days, just as in our calendar. This 365-day year was called *haab.* The sacred calendar was called *tzolkin.* It contained 260 days. The days of the *tzolkin* marked the ceremonial life of the people.

If we imagine both years as revolving cogged wheels, with a *tzolkin*-day cog meshing always with a *haab*-day cog, then we can see how the Maya knew what day in the ceremonial year fell on what day in the civil year. Because the imaginary cogged wheels were endlessly going around, the same two days would mesh once every fifty-two civil years.

There were nine divisions of time. They were as follows:

kin — a day
uinal — a month of 20 days
tun — a year of 18 *uinals* (360 days)
katun — 20 *tuns*, or years (7,200 days)
baktun — 20 *katuns* (144,000 days)
pictun — 20 *baktuns* (2,880,000 days)
calabtun — 20 *pictuns* (57,600,000 days)
kinchiltun — 20 *calabtuns* (1,152,000,000 days)
alautun — 20 *kinchiltuns* (23,040,000,000 days)

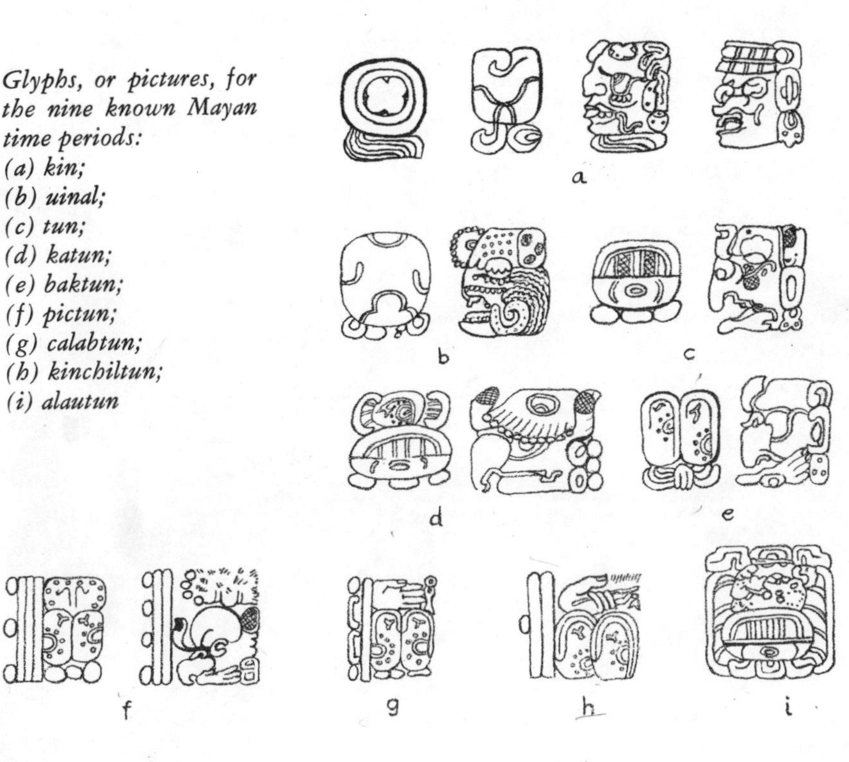

Glyphs, or pictures, for the nine known Mayan time periods:
(a) kin;
(b) uinal;
(c) tun;
(d) katun;
(e) baktun;
(f) pictun;
(g) calabtun;
(h) kinchiltun;
(i) alautun

Notice that the year time-divisions of the Maya are based on the number 20.

To study astronomy, the priests needed another tool: mathematics. Here again, they probably borrowed from the Olmecs, but their achievements in this field are amazing. The Maya understood the value of zero, or nothing. They also understood place-value notation, or positional arithmetic. We use place-value notation when we write numbers today. For example, if we write the number one (1), each zero we add to the right of it increases the number by ten times, 10; 100; 1,000.

The simple form of Mayan number-writing involved three symbols: the picture of a shell, or possibly some other symbol, for zero; the dot • ; and the bar ——. The dot equals one, and the bar equals five. Here is the count to nineteen:

0 1 2 3 4

5 6 7 8 9

10 11 12 13 14

15 16 17 18 19

The Mayan system was vigesimal: that is, it was based on twenty. The numbers were read vertically, from bottom to top, not horizontally. To go beyond nineteen, we must think in groups of twenty. Here are four numbers in Mayan notation:

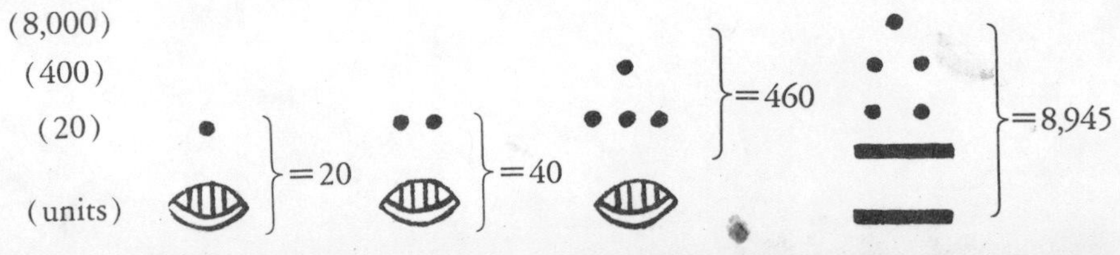

We read the last right-hand number as follows: there is one unit of 8,000; two units of 400, equaling 800; seven units of 20, or 7 x 20 = 140; and finally one bar, or 5, making a grand total of 8,945.

This number system is fairly simple, but the Maya also used head glyphs, or pictures of heads, which signified different numbers. For example, the head glyph for the number 1 looks like this:

Head glyph for the number 1

Scholars can read these strange-looking pictures of heads, but they are still at a loss to read most other Mayan hieroglyphic writing. It is felt, however, that these other glyphs record religious offerings and ceremonial events.

The Maya had hundreds of gods. Among the more important were Itzamna, the Lord of the Heavens and of Day and Night; Chac, the god of the four cardinal compass points. The Chac or Chacs were also rain gods who caused rain when they sprinkled water from gourds, or caused floods by throwing down the gourds when they were angry.

Other important gods included Yum Kaax, the God of Corn; Ah Puch, the God of Death; Ixchel, the Moon Goddess; Ixtab, the Goddess of Suicide; and a host of dieties of the sky, sun, Venus, wind, heaven, and hell, as well as the God of War, Sudden Death, and Human Sacrifice. In addition to these there were gods for all the periods of time.

The Maya believed that man was made from corn. They also believed that the earth had been destroyed several times by great floods. There were thirteen heavens and nine underworlds. These were all in layers, with a god for each layer. People who committed suicide went to the very top layer of heaven. Those deserving severe punishment went to the lowest hell, called Mitnal, which was freezing cold.

Sacrifice played an important part in Mayan religion in the later times. Then blood was essential to the gods, particularly to the rain gods. Priests and commoners alike pierced their tongues and ears, smearing their blood on the idols. It was thought that blood sacrifices would bring rain. Human sacrifices became more and more common during the last years of the Mayan empire. They took place when disasters struck — when there was no rain, when crops

From left to right, Mayan likenesses of Yum Kaax, the Corn God; Ah Puch, God of Death; a mask of the Rain God Chac, with his long nose

The Sacred Well at Chichén Itzá, where human beings were sacrificed to appease the gods. The victims plunged sixty feet to the water below

failed, or when plagues, foreign invasion, or other calamity struck. Generally the human sacrifices were made either by cutting the heart out of the victims, by throwing short spears at a painted area on the victim's chest, or by flinging the victim into a *cenote,* or sacred well.

The most famous Well of Sacrifice is at Chichén Itzá, where victims were cast into the dark sacred waters sixty feet below. This fantastic ceremony attracted thousands of people from miles around. They came to see the brilliant procession march from the Temple of Kukulkan to the well's edge. The sacrificed humans were not usually tied, as it was considered an honor to be chosen for the ceremony. This took place in the morning, and if the victim survived the fall and did not drown by noontime, he was pulled out of the water and asked what message he brought back from the gods. No matter what he answered, he was treated well thereafter because he was thought to be partly divine.

The Sacred Well at Chichén Itzá has been dredged and the bones of about fifty persons have been found. Those sacrificed were believed to go to the highest level of the Mayan heaven.

Into the same spirit-filled waters the awestruck Indians cast gold jewelry, copper bells, jade beads, pottery, knives, and other valuables, to please the gods.

When the priest-rulers of two powerful cities quarreled, war often followed. Wars usually were fought after the corn was harvested, because the warriors were also farmers. There were two war captains. One, the *nacom,* was elected for three years, while the other, the *batab,* held his title for life. Armies were formed and trained in the villages. Among the weapons used were spears, war clubs, flint knives, slings for hurling rocks, and later, bows and arrows. The Mayans also had a secret weapon: they threw hornets' nests into the enemy lines.

If the weapons were simple, the costumes were not. The warriors painted their bodies and wore elaborate headdresses, feathered capes, and jewelry. Drums, and horns made of conch shells furnished additional sound for each of their screaming attacks. The object of war was to capture prisoners, not to kill. Important prisoners were sacrificed; unimportant ones became slaves. Wars usually ended when each side had enough prisoners, or when it was planting time.

TRADE AND COMMUNICATION

The Maya were great traders. Merchants, called *ppolm* in Mayan, were important enough to be exempt from taxes. Yucatán traders traveling to the highlands of Guatemala brought back jade, obsidian, and the feathers of the rare and beautiful quetzal bird, found only in the highlands of Central America. The highland Maya traded for honey, cotton cloth, salt, and scores of other items. Trade was not confined to the Mayan people alone. The town of Xicalanco, on the west side of the Yucatán Peninsula, was a trading center for Mexican tribes such as the Toltecs and the Aztecs.

Because of frequent scuffles among the city-states, merchants led hazardous lives. Many conducted their business under the protective eye and arm of their own private armies or navies.

Carved jades. The head and necklace were found lying on the Red Jaguar Throne at Chichén Itzá. The jade pendant shows a high priest seated on a throne. The lines in front of his mouth mean that he is talking.

Trade was carried across the waters to the nearer islands of the Caribbean, all along the coast of Yucatán, and possibly as far south as Panama. Merchants used great open canoes, often as long as forty feet, and the paddles were manned by slaves. The peoples of coastal cities such as Tulum were fishermen as well as farmers. They traded dried fish, turtle eggs, and conch shells.

Marvelous wide roads ran between important cities. These roads were raised from two to eight feet above the surrounding countryside. Made of stone, they were paved with a smooth lime cement, and ran straight as arrows for miles. They were built and maintained by the common citizens. At intervals along them were resting-houses or wayside inns for weary foot travelers. These roads never felt the turn of a wheel or the stomp of a hoof, for all traveling was done on foot. The Maya never understood the idea of the wheel, nor did they have horses or other pack animals.

Because there were no pack animals, everything that was going overland to market was carried on the backs of the Indians, often for a distance of thirty or forty miles. Usually the entire family made the journey, and even the smallest child carried something.

The marketplaces were the great plazas and courts of the cities. One of the most famous of these is in the Court of a Thousand Columns at the base of the Temple of the Warriors in Chichén Itzá. This area is approximately four and a half acres in size. Here a crush of people probably bought and sold, bartered, haggled, and argued over mountains of vegetables, fruits, meat, fishes, tools, pottery, animals, birds, feathers — and even people. For slave trading

Although not many are left standing, colonnades once completely surrounded the 4½-acre, open-air market at Chichén Itzá. This area, at the base of the Temple of the Warriors, is often called the Court of the Thousand Columns

was a big business. The slaves were usually the unfortunate prisoners of war and the former citizens of nearby cities.

There was no money system comparable to those of modern nations. Cacao beans were rare and precious, and they were often used as money. Jade, quetzal-bird feathers, stone beads, and slaves were also used in place of money. The Maya had counterfeiters, too. To cheat a customer or merchant, they sometimes filled empty cacao-bean shells with dirt. Those traders who didn't want to be swindled learned to bite or pinch each bean to test its solidness. According to Bishop Landa, a slave was worth one hundred solid cacao beans.

THE ARTS

The Maya were remarkable painters, sculptors, potters, and weavers. The best example of Mayan painting is in the city of Bonampak, which means "painted walls" in Mayan. (We do not know the ancient name of this city.) There, in 1946, Giles G. Healey, a photographer and explorer, discovered a building with three doors and three rooms, deep in the jungle of the Usumacinta Valley. The walls of each room were covered with paintings, or murals, showing handsomely dressed priests and lords attended by servants; a brilliant battle scene; elaborate ceremonies; dances; and a human sacrifice. These were the first paintings to show Mayan life plainly without confusing ornaments, flourishes, and symbols. The brightly colored paintings had been preserved for more than eleven hundred years by water dripping steadily through the limestone roof and forming a protective lime coating over the walls.

Recently, in a little ceremonial city called Multunchic, near Uxmal and Kabah, other similar wall paintings have been discovered. These, too, are pictures of scenes, rather than symbols.

To begin a mural, the artist outlined the figures in red. The background was then painted in. Next, the details of the person's dress were filled in, and finally each figure was outlined in black. The artists were masters at making paints from minerals, and occasionally from plants.

The most famous color is known as Mayan blue. The origin of

Sacrificial victims, from the mural in Room 2 at Bonampak. Over the elaborate headdresses are examples of Mayan writing. These "speech scrolls" indicate that the person is speaking

this beautiful blue is unknown. It is thought to come from a blue mineral clay. The red and pink colors were made from red iron oxide; yellows from ocher; dark browns from asphalt or bitumen; and black from carbon. Green resulted from mixing blue and yellow.

In the earlier cities, stone carving is everywhere. Most of it is in the form of stelae and altars. Stelae — great stones, the largest of which is over thirty feet high — are carved with the figure of a man and with date glyphs. They were time markers, and were erected and dedicated at the ends of *katuns* (twenty years), half *katuns* (ten years), and sometimes *hotuns* (five years). Before the Indians carved in stone, they may have carved their dates on wooden stelae, though this cannot be proved because wood would have rotted by now. There are, however, carved wooden lintels —

Within the walls of Structure 39 at Tikal is a thick limestone shaft called Stela 22, or the Corn God Stela. Carved on it is a human figure sowing corn. Buried beneath this stela, nine obsidian stones and other offerings were found

pieces that run across the tops of door openings. Idols and masks were also carved in wood. Most generally used for carving was sapodilla, the very hard wood of the chicle tree.

In the later cities the walls and steps of temples and palaces bore stone carvings as well as stucco modeling. Faces, figures, and glyphs were deftly molded from a kind of plaster and then frequently painted.

Beautiful examples of clay modeling have been found in a cemetery on the island of Jaina. The little statues of priests, women, warriors, chieftains, and other people are masterly.

It is hard to imagine that such fine pottery could have been made without a potter's wheel, but apparently it was. Mayan artists simply shaped lumps of clay, or took strands of it in their hands and coiled them round and round. Smoothed and shaped, the clay became many things: three-footed bowls; whistles in the shape of animals; platters; incense burners; cooking pots; jars; and vases. Some of these pieces were painted, stamped, or engraved, but many were not. Later, some of the clay figures seem to have been made in a mold. In addition, Mayan artists carved jade into jewelry and idols. In later times, they worked metals such as copper and gold.

The Maya liked music and dancing, but these activities apparently had their place only in religious ceremonies. Music was the background for chanting prayers, for relating the myths and legends of the people, or for ceremonial dancing. There were no stringed instruments, but only percussion and wind instruments. Drums were made from hollow logs, tortoise shells, and even clay,

This jade statuette was found under the stairway of a temple at Uaxactún, and weighs 11½ pounds. Its eyes are rectangular and painted red.

Statue of a god, at Copán

in every imaginable size and shape. Other rhythm instruments included bells, gourd rattles, and bones that were tapped or rubbed against each other. Human leg bones were used as rhythm and melody instruments. Flutes also carried the melody, as did trumpets, which were made from conch shells, wood, and clay.

Music was probably more rhythmic than melodic, as its place was secondary to dancing. According to Spanish chronicles, if a player missed a beat the punishment was severe. The dancers, sometimes numbering in the hundreds, also were punished if they missed a step. There were groups of men dancers and of women dancers, but the two very rarely danced together. Some ritual dances hopefully brought rain; others symbolized the hunter and the hunted; still others pictured wars and daily happenings. According to the murals at Bonampak, the dancers wore magnificent costumes. Keeping a three-foot-high feathered headdress in place while performing a war dance must have been difficult, too.

No examples of Mayan weaving remain, though woven materials are shown in murals and on carvings. But in the Guatemalan highlands today weaving is done much as it was centuries ago, and many of the beautiful pieces closely resemble those pictured by the ancients. The Maya grew and processed their own cotton and prepared their own dyes.

Another amazing art was the making of feather mosaics, weaving many-colored feathers into the cotton. Sometimes, instead, the feathers were tied in by cords, or pasted onto the fabric. Only priests, chiefs, and important warriors could afford to adorn themselves with quetzal-feather mosaics, because of the high cost. Helmets, jackets, and breechclouts were made of the quetzal's golden-green feathers. Mounted on long poles, feathers were also used to keep mosquitoes and flies away from the noblemen.

The Mayan sculpture shows intricately designed body tattooing, which must also have been an art. The design was carefully cut into the skin, and variously colored dyes were rubbed into the individual cuts. Healing must have been a real problem, and the whole process must have been painful. The patterns, following the curves of the face and body, were ornamental, even artistic, but they may have been enjoyed more by onlookers than by their owners.

A cross-eyed Mayan priest wearing an elaborate headdress. The figure is carved in bone

THE CLASSICAL CITIES

Scholars divide Mayan history several ways, but we need only talk about the *Classical* and *Toltec*, or *Post-Classical, Periods*. The *Classical Period* drew to a close around A.D. 850. During its years the cities of Tikal, Copán, Piedras Negras, and Yaxchilán rose to splendor. This, too, was the time of great achievement: arithmetic, writing, astronomy, and the arts flourished.

Among the greatest works of the Maya were their cities. Classical Mayan cities were not inhabited, but were centers of religious ceremony. The people lived beyond the city limits at various distances, according to their social standing. Nearest the temples and plazas were the homes of the priests and nobility; next were the middle- or merchant-class dwellings: and finally came the houses of the peasants. No trace of these dwellings has been found, because they were made of perishable materials, not of stone.

Imagine hundreds, even thousands, of workers hauling, pushing, and pulling tons of stone and dirt to make the gigantic earth platforms on which the pyramid-temples stood. A large number of the Mayan buildings were placed on top of these earth platforms. And this tremendous job was accomplished without the help of draft animals and wheeled vehicles.

During the work, seven-foot-high bonfires, topped with chunks of limestone, were lit. The heat of these fires acted on the stone to produce a lime powder, which was the basic material of Mayan cement.

Farmers and slaves swarmed in the forests cutting trees to keep the bonfires going, while at the building site the stone pyramid-temple took its final form. Lime stucco, or cement, was applied to the cut stone building blocks so that the surface was very smooth. In some cities the stones were carved beforehand. In others, the artisans worked only with the stucco, modeling and molding it in a thousand strange and beautiful shapes. Finally, the pyramid-temple was painted.

Classical Mayan cities were brilliantly colored, not gleaming white or clean gray as they are today. Weather and time have washed away the outside colors, but color still remains on many inside murals, as well as on countless sculptured walls, steps, and columns.

No one now knows how long it took to build a pyramid-temple, but work probably went on for five years or more. And all the time the cities themselves were being added to or rebuilt over and over.

A finished temple was consecrated by priests, who dedicated it to the service of a particular god. The building was dated in the picture writing of the Maya, just as today we inscribe the year of completion on many of our buildings, bridges, and tunnels.

We may ask, Why did these ancient people build such magnificent cities if they did not plan to live in them? The answer is, They were built to please the gods and to win favor from them.

Tikal

Deep in the lowlands of Petén is the largest, perhaps the oldest, and surely the greatest of all Mayan cities. Rising from a rainy green jungle, this city covers many miles. Its outer limits are still unmapped. Although archeologists have been working here for years, most of Tikal is still untouched. What appear to be hills covered with vines, mosses, grass, and trees are actually pyramids and temples, buried for now and perhaps for all time.

Columns of stinging ants march single file beside a stone causeway; spider monkeys, parrots, toucans, and wild turkeys rule the orchid-filled treetops. For twelve centuries the sounds they have made have replaced those of the chanting priests and ceremonial dancers. Heat and moisture make things grow in the rain forest, and when the last Maya abandoned this great city, the jungle moved in quickly.

In 1696, ruined Tikal was rediscovered by Father Andrés de Avendaño, a Spanish missionary to the Indians. The city has six huge pyramid-temples, two of which face each other across a great plaza. The Temple of the Giant Jaguar, with its pyramid, is sixteen stories high. On its top is a single door leading to three thick-walled rooms, which are placed one in back of another. An enormous roof comb, a crest of stone and stucco, adds more height, and must have made the temple seem even more awesome to the Mayan farmers.

Across the plaza the facing pyramid-temple is decorated with many sculptured masks. It is called the Temple of the Masks, and

The Temple of the Giant Jaguar at Tikal. This temple has an elaborate roof comb which shows a seated high priest with huge earplugs and an elegant headdress. The temple, built in approximately A.D. *750, has been partly restored by the University of Pennsylvania*

is twelve feet lower than the Temple of the Giant Jaguar, which is 143 feet high.

On the south side of the plaza are two rows of stelae. Behind them a five-step staircase runs the length of the plaza and leads to sixteen more temples. This whole group of pyramids and temples is only one of dozens in Tikal.

In 1962, a tunnel dug in the Temple of the Giant Jaguar led to a tomb containing beautiful jade, pearl, and shell jewelry; a four-inch-high jade figurine; many pieces of painted pottery; an alabaster vase; and scores of other rich offerings. It is hoped that the finds made at Tikal during each archeological season will help solve the many mysteries that still surround the Mayan civilization.

The Red Stela was discovered by the archeologist Edwin M. Shook of the University of Pennsylvania in Temple 34, the first temple to be excavated at Tikal. It is painted red and was found broken in two

Copán

About one hundred and twenty years ago, the first archeologist of the Maya came to the bank of the Copán River and "saw directly opposite a stone wall, with furze growing out of the top. Perhaps a hundred feet high, it ran north and south along the river." John Lloyd Stephens, with his artist-friend Frederick Catherwood, was looking at the second greatest Mayan city, Copán. Captivated by its forest-hidden terraces, carved stelae, sculptured staircase, and pyramids, Stephens bought Copán for fifty dollars.

Ranging over seventy-five acres, this city was the center of science. Its astronomers calculated the length of time between eclipses. To celebrate their discovery, they built a temple in A.D. 756. This is one of the three most important buildings in Copán's main section.

Another temple is dedicated to the planet Venus. A third is at the top of the famous Hieroglyphic Stairway. There are sixty-two steps in the thirty-three-foot-wide staircase. Each riser is carved, and there are about two thousand hieroglyphic carvings in all.

Although Mayan dates have been deciphered, no one has been able to read these carved glyphs. In the middle of every twelfth step is a huge seated figure of a priest or god, while the ramp carvings on either side picture feathered serpents.

Nearby is the Jaguar Stairway. On either side of this are handsome stone jaguars which once had spots of shiny black obsidian.

The Hieroglyphic Stairway at Copán. John Lloyd Stephens thought that if the nearly two thousand glyphs on these stairs could be read they would reveal the entire history of the classical city of Copán

Copán is a maze of pyramids, temples, and plazas flanked by tiers of stone seats. One important group of buildings is seven miles away from the central section. This distance suggests that the city was surrounded by a large number of people.

Besides being the center of science, Copán was a great trading post. Situated farther south than any other Mayan city, it probably carried on a brisk trade with the people of Panama, who could work metals. In the base of one of the stelae, dedicated in A.D. 782, two tiny gold feet were found, separated from the rest of a figurine.

Palenque

Almost three hundred miles north and west of Copán are the ruins of Palenque. Here, in 1952, the Mexican archeologist Alberto Ruz Lhuillier made a startling discovery.

For nearly four seasons his workers had slowly taken tons of earth and stone from a stairway found beneath the floor of the Temple of the Inscriptions. They were now sixty feet down, almost to the base of the pyramid. Ruz had wondered why the stairway was filled in, and where it led. Now part of the answer lay before his eyes. There were the bones of six persons. Perhaps they had been sacrificed to serve some important person in his afterlife.

The workers carefully proceeded, cutting a hole through the rubble at one side of a huge stone slab. Ruz waited impatiently until the hole was made larger. Then he peered through it, into a burial

The burial crypt under the Temple of the Inscriptions at Palenque

chamber that had not been seen for over one thousand years.

Water, dripping over limestone for centuries, had formed glistening stalactites. On the walls of this eerie chapel were nine stucco figurines—possibly the nine gods of the underworld. A carved stone slab almost the size of the thirty-foot chamber lay over a tomb. When this five-ton covering was slowly raised by the workers, the polished stone lid of the tomb itself came into view. Beneath this lay the skeleton of the *halach uinic,* covered with jade ornaments and a jade mosaic mask. Pottery, jade figurines, and two magnificent stucco heads were found nearby.

The tomb might never have been discovered if Ruz had not wondered about the small holes in a flagstone in the temple floor far above. These were the fingerholes of a secret trap door, opening on the staircase.

Leading from the tomb up the stairs to the floor above was a hollow tube of stone and cement. This strange pipe was probably used by the priests to send and receive messages from the dead priest-king below.

Many of Palenque's pyramid-temples had elaborate roof combs. The wider doors and thinner walls of the buildings made them superior to those in most Mayan cities. On the walls were delicately modeled or carved figures of rulers, gods, slaves, quetzals, animals, and mythical beings. Here the art of stucco modeling reached its highest point.

The Temple of the Inscriptions at Palenque. A secret staircase in the core of this pyramid leads down to the famous tomb of a chieftain buried about A.D. *700*

REVOLT, MIGRATION, AND THE TOLTECS

The great Classical ceremonial cities of the Petén region had flourished for 570 years. But by A.D. 900 these centers were all but abandoned and left to ruin. Why? Archeologists have given a number of possible answers to this mystery. Some have thought that the soil could not supply enough food, and that the people moved away to avoid starvation. Others have suggested drought, earthquakes, plagues, invasion, and violent changes in climate.

In recent years, scholars have found a new explanation. Many of them believe that the peasants revolted against the priests. Over the years the priest group had grown larger, and so had the number of gods, rituals, and ceremonies. The priests had lost touch with the farmers, but their demands on them had grown. More work was required — and more corn, more temples and palaces — until at last the farmers rose up. There is plenty of evidence to support this idea. Many buildings have been left half finished, and no more stelae were erected after A.D. 909.

The strongest evidence may have been found in the cities of Tikal and Piedras Negras. A stela at Tikal was deliberately smashed. A sacred throne, a wall panel, and stelae were destroyed at Piedras Negras. These objects, once revered, only reminded the peasants of their servitude. Blind faith had turned to blind hate.

The revolts spread. Priests and officials were probably murdered. As time went on, the peasants found themselves without leaders.

For centuries they had been told what to do, and when, and how. Now they were alone with their newly won freedom. Work stopped on the temples. Slowly the jungle moved into the plazas, and vines mounted the temple steps. Gradually the people abandoned the cities.

Now comes a second mystery. What became of these two or three million people? For a time, scholars thought that they had moved north to Yucatán and had built new cities. But it is now known that the great northern cities were already there, and thriving. Probably there are three answers to the mystery. Some of the people stayed on, their way of life growing poorer and their numbers slowly dwindling. Some moved to the Guatemalan highlands. The remainder went north to the Mexican states now called Campeche, Yucatán, and Quintana Roo.

The mainstream of Mayan history turned northward to a low range of hills named Puuc, and to the Yucatán plain. In the hills and valleys of the Puuc area lay the splendid cities of Kabah, Labná, Sayil, and Uxmal. North of the Puuc Hills and to the east were the important cities of Mayapán, Dzibilchaltun, Izamal, Chichén Itzá, and Cobá.

The Petén immigrants had left behind them steaming rain forests, swamps, treeless plains, and a revolution. They found scrub trees, thick undergrowth pushing up from a parched plain, and a revolution — for the northern cities were in trouble, too.

The whole Mayan civilization shook to rid itself of the priesthood, and it was not alone, for the farming tribes of the Mexican mainland were trying to do the same thing. Throughout the Mayan country and the Valley of Mexico, the Classical Period drew to a violent close.

After A.D. 900, most of the Maya lived either in the Guatemalan highlands or in northern Yucatán. The people of the highlands evidently did not develop their civilization further. Those in Yucatán did, because of Mexican invaders called the Toltecs.

Tula, the capital of the Toltecs, was 45 miles from present-day Mexico City. Before A.D. 900, the Valley of Mexico had come under the rule of these vigorous and warlike people. They had a calendar, were pyramid-builders, and practiced many arts and crafts. Through trading they had come in contact with the Maya.

Carved on a rock cliff at Tula is a portrait of Quetzalcoatl (ket-sahl-COH-ahtl), with the name Ce Acatl and a hieroglyphic date corresponding to A.D. 968. Quetzalcoatl was the name given by the Toltecs to a god and to certain priest-kings. The Quetzalcoatl who changed Mayan history was known as Ce Acatl Topiltzin. Because history and legend have mixed the story of this priest-king with the god of the same name, we do not really know what happened. But the ancient chronicles say that after twenty-two years as ruler of the Toltecs, he exiled himself, and was followed by priests, chiefs, and some of his people.

The chronicles tell us that he entered Mayan country sometime between the years A.D. 987 and 1000. The Maya apparently offered little resistance to the invasion. Called Itzá by the conquered people, the Toltecs settled down at Chichén Itzá, "the well of the Itzá."

The Maya of the Guatemala highlands were invaded at about the same time.

What became of Quetzalcoatl, or Kukulkan, as he was known in the Mayan language, is not known. Some say he sailed away toward the sunrise on a raft made of intertwined snakes. According to legend, he disappeared on Ce Acatl, the date on which he was born, and promised to return on another Ce Acatl.

By A.D. 1000, the Toltec warriors and the priest class had full control of Yucatán. The Quetzalcoatl of the invasion had departed. He was a peaceful thinker who would not have approved of the bloodthirsty gods and priests and the religious ceremonies involving human sacrifice. But, instead of weakening the Mayan civilization, the Toltec invaders brought new life.

The Toltec Quetzalcoatl, who later became the Mayan god Kukulkan. The background shows a feathered serpent. Feathered serpents and jaguars are common designs in Toltec art

A jaguar carved on the side of the Tzompantli, or skull rack, at Chichén Itzá

CITIES OF THE NORTH

Shortly after the Toltecs won control over the Maya, they forced the people in the Puuc area to move down onto the Yucatán plain, near the *cenotes*, the natural pools of the limestone area. The Toltecs probably reasoned that they could keep a closer eye on the farmers if they were not scattered among the Puuc Hills. Furthermore, the water supply in the hills was a constant problem.

The abandoned cities of Kabah, Labná, Sayil, and Uxmal, as well as less important centers, now fell to ruin. These four major Puuc cities had been built close together. They strung along, north to south, for approximately twenty miles, with Labná off to the east of Sayil. A population of about 25,000 had formerly surrounded them.

The remains of the Puuc cities show they were vastly different from those in the west and south. There are fewer pyramid-temples, many more palaces, and very few stelae. The greater number of royal or civil buildings probably shows a move away from priest rule toward civilian rule. In addition, the buildings are generally made of concrete, with a veneer of beautifully cut and fitted stones.

Nothing has been found in the Petén area to compare with the magnificent palace at Sayil, which contains one hundred rooms. But, dark and windowless, the rooms were separated by thick stone walls, and each chamber was small and damp. Instead of doors, drop or pull curtains closed their openings.

The narrowness of most Mayan rooms is caused by their corbel arch. In such an arch the sides gradually angle in toward each other and are joined by a capstone.

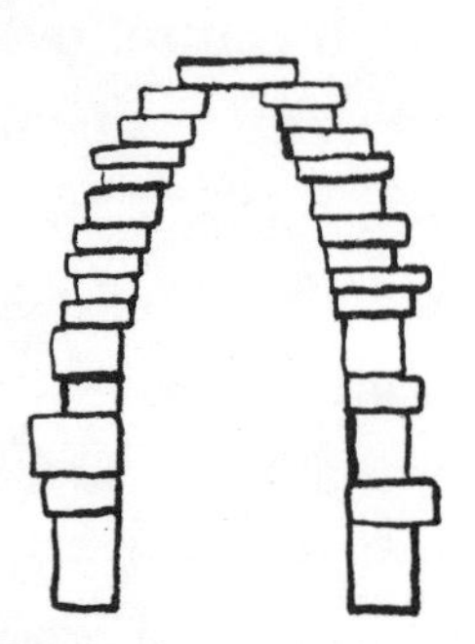

A corbel arch, with capstone

With an arch of this kind, the roof would have collapsed if the walls had been set too far apart.

In Yucatán, the Toltecs introduced the idea of resting the arch's vault on columns instead of on thick, damp walls, and the rooms became larger and airier.

Uxmal

The most beautiful city of the Puuc area is Uxmal. Dominating the city's six main building groups is the Palace of the Governor, so called by the Spaniards. This stands on top of a triple terrace fifty feet high, which covers five acres of land. The building is long and shallow, and contains twenty-four rooms. Its four sides are decorated with approximately twenty thousand perfectly fitted pieces of stone, some of which weigh several hundred pounds. These beautifully carved and fitted mosaic walls are one of the greatest native works of art in the Americas.

Not far from the Palace is the Nunnery Quadrangle. Here four buildings face a large court. Their ornate walls of carved and fitted stone depict rain gods, serpents, latticework, and other objects. The doorways of the four buildings are odd-numbered: five, seven, nine, and eleven.

Nearby is the Pyramid of the Dwarf, or the House of the Magician, or the House of the Adivino. It is called by three names. This curious pyramid has two rounded ends, which make it oval, and its stairs are extremely steep.

According to native folklore there was once an old witch who longed for a son. She was told to put an iguana egg in her house. She did this, and soon the egg hatched a beautiful baby boy. The delighted witch raised her son carefully, but when the handsome and brilliant boy was eight years old he stopped growing.

Many years later, the witch's dwarfed son came upon a musical

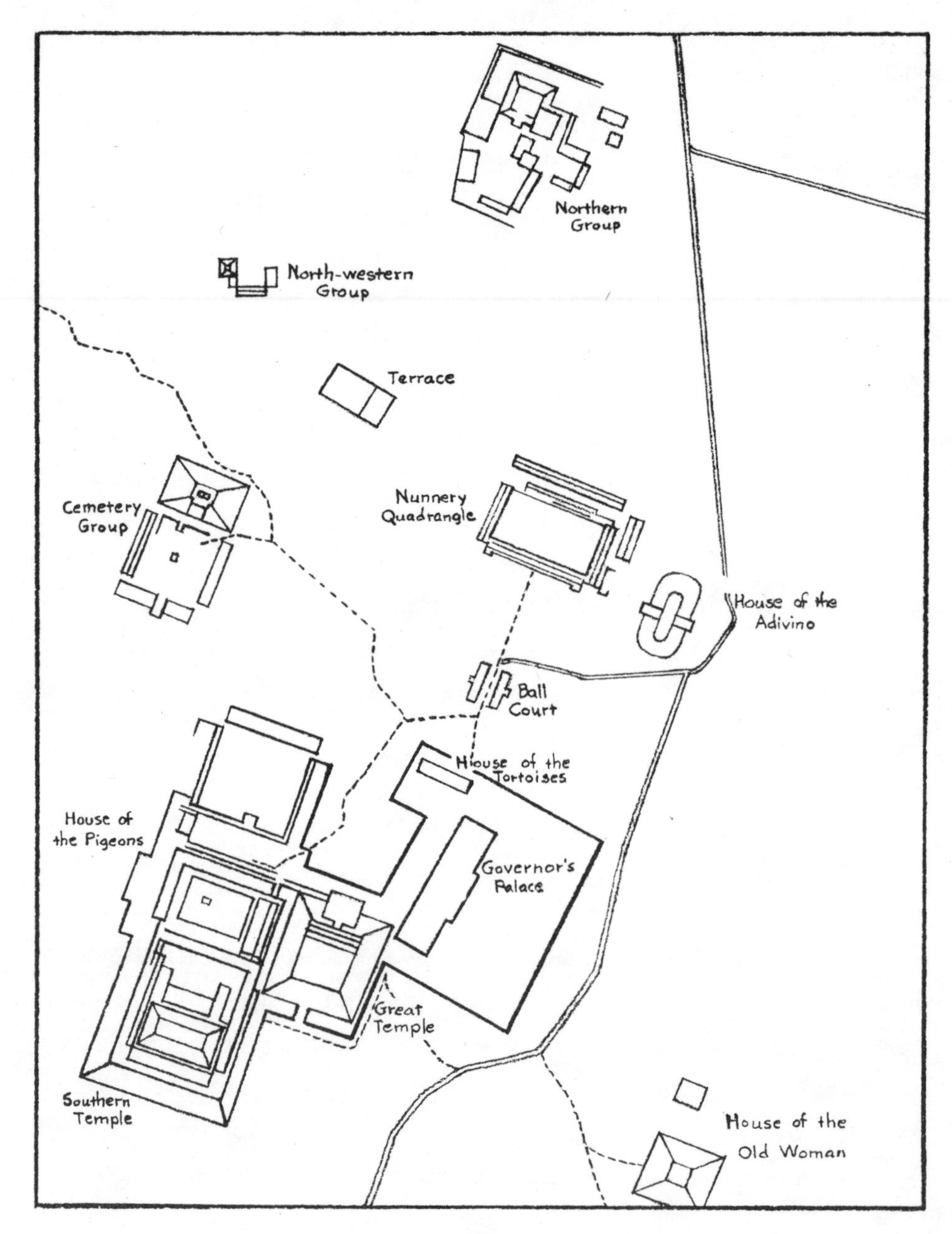

Plan of the city of Uxmal

Two sides of the Nunnery Quadrangle at Uxmal. Each of the buildings on the four sides of this court is of a different height and is decorated in a different way

instrument in the forest. It was thought by the people that whoever could play this instrument would become the next king of Uxmal. When the dwarf began playing lovely music on it, everyone in the whole city heard him. Naturally the reigning king of Uxmal wished to remain in power, so he challenged the dwarf to two tasks. First, the dwarf, to prove he was worthy, must build the tallest, fairest pyramid-temple in all Uxmal — in one night. This he did; it is the Pyramid of the Dwarf. Second, three bags of coconuts were to be broken, one after the other, on his head. If the dwarf survived, the crafty king, in turn, was to have three bags of coconuts broken on *his* head.

Now the old witch had devised a way of protecting her son by making him a stone cap, over which she placed a wig. Each of the three bags of coconuts crashed down on the dwarf's head. Nothing happened. But the first bag that broke over the king's head brought his death. The people of the city rejoiced; they had a new king. The dwarf-magician ruled them wisely for many years.

Today, in the woods near the Pyramid of the Dwarf, there is a leaning statue of an ugly woman holding a snake. At the bottom of this statue is a tiny figure, crouching as a bag descends on his head.

Kabah

Nine miles southeast of Uxmal is the second largest Puuc city, Kabah. A thousand years ago a causeway joined these two centers. The triumphal arch at Kabah marks its starting place.

Three groups of buildings have been freed of scrub trees and earth at Kabah, though many others are still mounds. Most unusual of the three is the Palace of the Masks, standing on a low platform. Running along the face of this building are dozens of stone masks of the Rain God Chac. The nose of each is long and coiled, and resembles the trunk of an elephant. Most of these trunks have been broken off.

Between the years A.D. 800 and 900, Kabah was probably sur-

The nose of the Rain God Chac is here used as a step leading to another chamber in the Palace of the Masks at Kabah

rounded by a large number of people. Because of the six-month droughts, common in the Puuc Hills, the Palace of the Masks may have been built as a special "appeal in stone" to Chac, the God of Rain.

Sayil

Sayil lies partly in two modern Mexican states: Yucatán and Campeche. Its most beautiful building, the Palace, has three stories, with the top two set back like stepped terraces. A gigantic staircase leads to the three levels. The Palace walls bear the Chac mask as well as descending gods, and monsters with alligator-like tails. The columns have top parts much like those of ancient Greece.

Another temple, called the Mirador, sits on top of a high pyramid. From this height it can be seen that nearly all Sayil's former grandeur is now mostly rubble.

Labná

Carved on the trunk-nose of the god Chac at Labná is a glyph date that corresponds to A.D. 869. This city is most famous for its lovely Arch. Here, carved in stone, are depicted the simple thatched houses of the Maya. On either side of the Arch's gateway are two small rooms. Nearby is a great pyramid with rounded ends, and a temple with a roof comb.

The Labná Palace is situated at the end of a raised ceremonial road which connects it with buildings near the Arch. This palace is a series of buildings joined together, and built at different times. It was probably Labná's government center. Today, a few of its rooms are used to accommodate overnight guests, as this is the only haven in many miles of wild, dry jungle.

Tulum

Located on the east coast of Yucatán, Tulum, unlike most Mayan cities, was walled and fortified. In many places the walls were twenty feet thick and fifteen feet high, and were about eight hun-

The beautiful Palace at Sayil has not been restored. Its construction, typical of the Puuc area, is of concrete faced with thin, finely-cut stones

The Arch at Labná. Roads joined the four great ceremonial cities of Uxmal, Labná, Sayil, and Kabah. The temple-pyramid in the background, topped by a huge roof comb, is called the Mirador. The pyramid has rounded ends just as the House of the Magician at Uxmal has

dred yards long. Enemies would have had to enter the city through five narrow gates, which could have been defended easily by only a few soldiers.

The city stands on a high, cactus-covered cliff above the Caribbean Sea. Facing the ocean is the Castillo, the most important building at Tulum. Both the city and its temple face east. One can imagine the high priests of Zama — for this was Tulum's ancient name — facing the morning sun and invoking the gods' blessings for the day. Zama means "the dawn" and Tulum means "walled."

The Castillo of the walled city of Tulum rests at the edge of the Caribbean Sea

Part of a mural from the Temple of the Frescoes at Tulum

A stela dates Tulum as early as A.D. 564, but the city's history is almost unknown. In 1518, men aboard four Spanish ships commanded by Juan de Grijalva sighted the walls. One member of the expedition wrote, "the city of Seville would not have struck us as larger or better."

Two shipwrecked Spaniards from a previous expedition had been held as slaves by Kinich, Lord of Tulum, after barely escaping being killed and eaten. One of these two men, Gerónimo de Aguilar, was rescued later by Cortes, but the other, Gonzalo de Guerrero, married a Mayan chieftain's daughter and became an honored war captain. He led the Indians in battle against his own countrymen.

Another important building in Tulum is the Temple of the Frescoes. Here the painted murals show rain gods and corn gods and serpent designs which are something like those of the Toltecs. Tulum has many things in common with the Mexican cities, even though it dates back to classical times.

Dzibilchaltun

Not far north of Mérida, the present-day capital of Yucatán, is Dzibilchaltun. From its great mounds of rubble the excavators have discovered that this center was earlier and quite different from the Puuc cities. Archeologists are at work restoring Dzibilchaltun. Not long ago they rebuilt the Temple of the Seven Dolls, so called because seven clay dolls were found beneath its floors. Unlike most of the Mayan temples, this one had windows.

Nearby is a church erected by the Spaniards. It is built of many stones taken from the ruins of Dzibilchaltun, and on them faint traces of Mayan figures can still be seen.

The Temple of the Seven Dolls at Dzibilchaltun

THE LEAGUE OF MAYAPAN

During the eleventh century the Itzá took as their capital Chichén Itzá, which was rebuilt for the third time. The Mayan people may have felt friendly toward the invaders, because they helped them with the work. As time went on, Chichén came to look more and more like Tula, the former capital of the Toltecs.

The decorative Toltec designs such as warriors, jaguars, eagles, and human skulls were sculptured widely. The most important sign of Toltec influence, though, was the serpent column, symbol of Quetzalcoatl-Kukulkan.

The Itzá occupied Chichén for about two centuries, from approximately A.D. 987 to 1185. Native chronicles state that this, too, was the time of the League of Mayapán. The city-states of Uxmal, Chichén Itzá, and Mayapán supposedly ruled in alliance over Yucatán.

At this point, however, we do not have a clear picture of Mayan history. Archeologists say that Uxmal had already been abandoned and that Mayapán was built after Chichén had fallen. Some authorities suggest that Izamal, not Uxmal, may have been the third city in the triple alliance.

The Books of Chilam Balam help us with a wonderful story about a minor chief by the name of Hunac Ceel. This young man was watching a sacrifice at the Sacred Well in Chichén Itzá. All morning the silent natives and priests had stood pressed to the well's edge, awaiting the reappearance of the sacrificial victims. The dark

The famous feathered serpent columns on top of the pyramid bearing the Temple of the Warriors at Chichén Itzá. Because the feathered serpent is a Mexican image, we know that these strange columns were erected after the Toltec invasion

waters had been still since early morning; no one had returned with a divine message from the gods. Suddenly Hunac Ceel sprang to the temple platform and hurled himself into the waters sixty feet below. Seconds passed; the crowd was shocked motionless; then Hunac reappeared. He was hauled from the waters with the holy words that the gods had declared him king. Soon after, he chose Mayapán as his capital.

The story goes on to say that the ruler of Chichén Itzá, a certain Chac Xib Chac, stole the bride of Ah Ulil, chief of Izamal. Hunac Ceel assembled a great army and swooped down on Chichén. Chac Xib Chac was driven out, and Chichén fell, never to rise again.

One of the carved columns in the Court of the Thousand Columns at Chichén Itzá. The figure is a plumed warrior, and is probably an exact likeness of a real person

According to the chronicles, Hunac was an ambitious schemer. After successfully defending Ah Ulil's honor, Hunac turned on his ally, and Ah Ulil and Izamal fell, too. Hunac's strength lay in his corps of Mexican bodyguards with their devastating new weapon, the bow and arrow.

After this time, the lords of Chichén Itzá and of Izamal were obliged to live at Mayapán where they were hostages, with some power. The Cocom, the name Hunac gave his dynasty, ruled Yucatán for about two hundred and fifty years.

Mayapán was, then, the first real capital of the Maya. It was a walled fortress city, and it was lived in instead of being merely a city of temples. Its inhabitants were supported not so much by farming as by tributes paid by Mayan subjects. Within an area of less than two square miles about fifteen thousand people lived in some thirty-five hundred buildings.

The wall surrounding Mayapán was over twelve feet high, and often as thick. Within the city were a number of *cenotes* (wells); the houses of the lords were nearest these. In the city's center was a copy of the Temple of Kukulkan at Chichén Itzá, its four sides facing the cardinal points of the compass. The houses of the ruling families were located nearest the main plaza.

Mayapán contained the worst examples of Mayan architecture and the poorest pottery. The small number of temples indicates that religion had sunk to a low point. Buildings were constructed of badly cut stone, and mistakes were covered up with generous layers of stucco. Sometimes the stones were set in mud. Today

This strange clay figure found at Mayapán was used as an incense burner

Mayapán is mostly rubble. From what is left, the buildings appear to have been poor imitations of those found at Chichén.

Chichén Itzá

In contrast to Mayapán was the lovely city of Chichén Itzá. Here a great deal of restoration work has been done by archeologists, and we can see today how remarkable this city must have been.

The Temple of Kukulkan rises majestically from Yucatán's flat plain. The sides of this pyramid are a monument to time. There are four stairways, each with ninety-one steps. Four times ninety-one equals 364, and adding the upper platform level gives us 365, the number of days in the civil year. The nine terraces of the pyramid are divided into fifty-two panels, the correct number for the Toltec ceremonial calendar. In addition, the terraces were separated by stairs into eighteen sections, the number of months in the Mayan year.

Inside the Kukulkan pyramid is another pyramid with a secret room, which contained the famous Red Jaguar Throne. This full-

The Red Jaguar Throne was discovered at Chichén Itzá in 1937, by archeologists of the Carnegie Institution

The Chac Mool figure was introduced to the Maya by the Toltecs

sized stone jaguar was painted red, and it once had seventy-three spots of polished jade.

In front of the Red Jaguar Throne is a Chac Mool, a human figure carved in stone and lying on its back. A bowl, held on its stomach, received the still-beating hearts of sacrificed human victims. This particular Chac Mool had mother-of-pearl inlaid eyes, teeth, and fingernails.

Three hundred yards down a causeway from this pyramid-temple is the Sacred Well of Sacrifice. Nearby is the Temple of the Warriors. The upper part of this temple features plumed serpent columns. These stone snakes once supported a roof, while their open, fanged mouths rested on the floor. At the ground level is a corridor of many columns. They depict Toltec warriors. Many carvings at Chichén show Mexican warriors defeating the Maya.

For Mayan craftsmen engaged in stone carving, it must have been a bitter task to shape these figures.

Within the pyramid of the Temple of the Warriors, archeologists discovered the Temple of the Chac Mool. Here a round limestone box revealed a beautiful turquoise mosaic disk.

Chichén Itzá has a gigantic ball court, the largest of the city's seven, with the Jaguar Temple next to it. Nearby is the Tzompantli or "skull rack," where the skulls of sacrificial victims were placed on posts.

The Caracol, or Observatory, is another remarkable building. The round tower topping its high terrace has rectangular openings. When the sun and moon are sighted through them, they reveal certain astronomical information. With their aid, Mayan astronomers were able to calculate the time of the vernal equinox — March 21.

Not far from the Caracol is the Nunnery. The upper section of this building is decorated with stone Chac masks with elephant-style noses.

Notice that the same names appear for buildings found in many cities — the Nunnery, the Temple of the Jaguar, the Temple of the Frescoes, and others. The Spanish, over four hundred years ago, gave the ruined buildings names that made sense and had meaning to them. A host of buildings have been named by archeologists and natives, too. We do not know what the Maya called most of their cities, much less their buildings. Chichén, when it was first founded (probably A.D. 432), had another name.

In 1441, the Tutul Xiu, one-time rulers of Uxmal, revolted

The Caracol, or Observatory, at Chichén Itzá. Within the round tower walls is a spiral staircase leading to a small observatory. The Caracol has three openings in its thick walls. By sighting along the walls of these openings, the priest-astronomers made certain astronomical discoveries. For example, the opening on the west wall allowed them to figure the vernal equinox, March 21, when day and night are of equal length

against the Cocom. The Xiu claimed that the Cocom were selling Mayan people as slaves to the Mexican Indians. The Xiu won the battle, the Cocom were run off, and Mayapán was burned and looted. The Xiu led their own people away from Mayapán and founded a new capital with the prophetic name of Mani, which means in Mayan, "It is passed."

This, then, was the end of centralized government. Thereafter, the Maya were governed by petty chiefs. The cities of the north fell into disrepair. No new temples or pyramids were built. A sickness seems to have crept over the land. The people no longer cared.

DZOOC U MAAN U KINIL (Mayan) —THE DAY HAS ENDED

During the one hundred years from the fall of Mayapán until the Spanish conquest, the people of Yucatán were beset by wars, plagues, droughts, hurricanes, and what was probably an epidemic of smallpox. They had beaten back two Spanish attempts to conquer them, one in 1527, and the other from 1531 to 1535.

There is ample proof, too, that the leading tribes felt only hate for one another. At one time nearly fifty leaders of the Tutul Xiu nation requested permission from the Cocom to pass safely through their land to the Well of Sacrifice at Chichén Itzá (1536). They thought that such a pilgrimage with its sacrifices would lift the curse on the Maya, and that this act would surely meet with the wholehearted approval of the Cocom. The Cocom chief readily agreed. The Xiu party was met and lavishly entertained for four days; then suddenly the Cocom fell upon their guests and killed them. The Cocom had not forgotten what the Xiu had done at Mayapán three generations earlier.

The Quiché Maya in the Guatemalan highlands fell at about the same time Mayapán was sacked. There followed a struggle for power, and a series of tribal wars until, in 1524, the Spanish conquered Guatemala with the help of another Mayan tribe, the Cakchiquel, enemies of the Quiché.

Francisco de Montejo the Younger commanded only a small band of four hundred men in the final Spanish conquest of Yucatán from 1540 to 1546. But the Spanish had two weapons that struck fear in Mayan hearts: guns and horses. The Indians had never before seen either. Mostly, however, the Mayan civilization was already lost because its members were so divided among themselves.

Fifty miles from Tikal is a lake called El Petén. After the destruction of Mayapán, one powerful Itzá tribe had withdrawn from Yucatán to the shores of this lake and had built a city called Tayasal. Deep in the jungle, this last stronghold infuriated the Spanish by holding out for one hundred and fifty years following the conquest of Yucatán.

On March 13, 1697, Martín de Ursua, Spanish governor of Yucatán, crossed El Petén in a huge galley with some of his soldiers. In the gray of early morning they drew near Tayasal as canoes filled with Indians set out from the shore. Ursua's 108 men held their fire while their leader shouted a last appeal for surrender and peace. The Indians answered with a shower of arrows, which wounded two men. In a rage one wounded soldier fired his gun, and the other soldiers quickly followed.

In shallow water the Spaniards pressed their advantage by leaping overboard and pursuing the Itzá up the hill. It was not long before the two thousand Indian warriors were joined by Tayasal's other inhabitants, all vainly trying to swim to the opposite shore and safety.

The waters of El Petén ran red. The Mayan day had ended.

INDEX